THE
3 Q
JOURNAL

The Simple Daily Practice
to be a Happier and More Effective Human

***

Copyright and Disclaimer

How to Use The 3 Question Journal

I built this simple journal to help you track your **progress, gratitude, and focus.**

The 3 questions are:

1. What did I get done today?
2. What am I grateful for?
3. How will I win tomorrow?

They're intentionally open-ended, but also backed by research to help you be more effective in your work and fulfilled in your life.

Why Progress?

In *The Slight Edge*, author Jeff Olson defines success as **"the progressive realization of a worthy ideal."**

The "progressive realization" part is key; success is a cumulative, consistent process, not an overnight lucky break.

To me, progress means forward motion, or actively taking the steps to improve each day. It's one thing we can control.

And progress is universal; everyone can make progress toward their goals in some meaningful way, however small the steps may seem.

It turns out I'm not alone either. We're wired to seek progress; psychologists have found it to be a key factor in our overall happiness.

Even Tony Robbins calls it the "1-word secret to happiness," telling CNBC, "I always tell people if you want to know the secret to happiness, I can give it to you in one word: progress."

Why Gratitude?

It's easy to get caught up in all the things you have to do and all the problems that need solving.

But taking a moment to reflect on what you're thankful for is a helpful re-frame. The world's not all bad. Even on the worst days, we all have something to be grateful for.

And it's not a waste of time, either. Leading positive psychology researchers have found that people who keep a gratitude journal actually become happier than those who don't.

Practice noticing the positive.

Why Focus?

I've interviewed over 500 successful entrepreneurs on The Side Hustle Show.

One of the common threads is these business owners don't leave their schedules up to chance. Instead, they plan out their top priorities ahead of time, and take action.

John Lee Dumas called it "winning tomorrow today."

Itemizing out your next-day priorities lets you start you day in proactive made, instead of reacting to someone else's agenda. It helps you make progress toward your goals, instead of putting out fires.

My recommendation? Write down 1-3 things that will feel good to accomplish.

Taking the time to write down how you'll "win tomorrow" makes those tasks real and sets yourself up for success.

The Process

Answering these questions nightly isn't a huge time commitment or massive lifestyle shift. In fact, using this journal should take **less than 5 minutes a day.**

And based on my experience and interviews with hundreds of successful entrepreneurs, it's 5 minutes well spent.

My Guarantee

If you follow the guidelines and prompts in this journal, I guarantee you'll feel more satisfied and productive with your work after just 28 days.

If you don't, just send me a note (my contact info is at the end of the book), and I'll buy the journal back from you, no questions asked.

Claim Your Free Bonuses

In the spirit of improving not just your productivity, but your overall effectiveness, I put together an exclusive bonus package for users of *The 3 Question Journal*.

1. The Productivity Tip Sheet

I asked some of my most successful entrepreneurial friends for their favorite productivity tips and tricks.

The result is this Tip Sheet.

I don't expect you to try all of these–especially not all at once–but use the quick-to-implement suggestions on this list to re-energize and re-focus.

2. The Digital 3 Question Journal

Several readers requested a digital version of the journal to use with their tablet and stylus. If you're embracing a paperless lifestyle, this one is for you.

Plus, it includes two extra months of digital pages.

Grab them both free here:

3QuestionJournal.com/bonus

Date: _____

What did I get done today?

What am I grateful for?

How will I win tomorrow?

Date: _____

What did I get done today?

What am I grateful for?

How will I win tomorrow?

Date: _____

What did I get done today?

What am I grateful for?

How will I win tomorrow?

Date: _____

What did I get done today?

What am I grateful for?

How will I win tomorrow?

Date: _____

What did I get done today?

What am I grateful for?

How will I win tomorrow?

Date: _____

What did I get done today?

What am I grateful for?

How will I win tomorrow?

Date: _____

What did I get done today?

What am I grateful for?

How will I win tomorrow?

Date: _____

What did I get done today?

What am I grateful for?

How will I win tomorrow?

Date: _____

What did I get done today?

What am I grateful for?

How will I win tomorrow?

Date: _____

What did I get done today?

What am I grateful for?

How will I win tomorrow?

Date: _____

What did I get done today?

What am I grateful for?

How will I win tomorrow?

Date: _____

What did I get done today?

What am I grateful for?

How will I win tomorrow?

Date: _____

What did I get done today?

What am I grateful for?

How will I win tomorrow?

Date: _____

What did I get done today?

What am I grateful for?

How will I win tomorrow?

Date: _____

What did I get done today?

What am I grateful for?

How will I win tomorrow?

Date: _____

What did I get done today?

What am I grateful for?

How will I win tomorrow?

Date: _____

What did I get done today?

What am I grateful for?

How will I win tomorrow?

Date: _____

What did I get done today?

What am I grateful for?

How will I win tomorrow?

Date: _____

What did I get done today?

What am I grateful for?

How will I win tomorrow?

Date: _____

What did I get done today?

What am I grateful for?

How will I win tomorrow?

Date: _____

What did I get done today?

What am I grateful for?

How will I win tomorrow?

Date: _____

What did I get done today?

What am I grateful for?

How will I win tomorrow?

Date: _____

What did I get done today?

What am I grateful for?

How will I win tomorrow?

Date: _____

What did I get done today?

What am I grateful for?

How will I win tomorrow?

Date: _____

What did I get done today?

What am I grateful for?

How will I win tomorrow?

Date: _____

What did I get done today?

What am I grateful for?

How will I win tomorrow?

Date: _____

What did I get done today?

What am I grateful for?

How will I win tomorrow?

Date: _____

What did I get done today?

What am I grateful for?

How will I win tomorrow?

Date: _____

What did I get done today?

What am I grateful for?

How will I win tomorrow?

Date: _____

What did I get done today?

What am I grateful for?

How will I win tomorrow?

Date: _____

What did I get done today?

What am I grateful for?

How will I win tomorrow?

Date: _____

What did I get done today?

What am I grateful for?

How will I win tomorrow?

Date: _____

What did I get done today?

What am I grateful for?

How will I win tomorrow?

Date: _____

What did I get done today?

What am I grateful for?

How will I win tomorrow?

Date: _____

What did I get done today?

What am I grateful for?

How will I win tomorrow?

Date: _____

What did I get done today?

What am I grateful for?

How will I win tomorrow?

Date: _____

What did I get done today?

What am I grateful for?

How will I win tomorrow?

Date: _____

What did I get done today?

What am I grateful for?

How will I win tomorrow?

Date: _____

What did I get done today?

What am I grateful for?

How will I win tomorrow?

Date: _____

What did I get done today?

What am I grateful for?

How will I win tomorrow?

Date: _____

What did I get done today?

What am I grateful for?

How will I win tomorrow?

Date: _____

What did I get done today?

What am I grateful for?

How will I win tomorrow?

Date: _____

What did I get done today?

What am I grateful for?

How will I win tomorrow?

Date: _____

What did I get done today?

What am I grateful for?

How will I win tomorrow?

Date: _____

What did I get done today?

What am I grateful for?

How will I win tomorrow?

Date: _____

What did I get done today?

What am I grateful for?

How will I win tomorrow?

Date: _____

What did I get done today?

What am I grateful for?

How will I win tomorrow?

Date: _____

What did I get done today?

What am I grateful for?

How will I win tomorrow?

Date: _____

What did I get done today?

What am I grateful for?

How will I win tomorrow?

Date: _____

What did I get done today?

What am I grateful for?

How will I win tomorrow?

Date: _____

What did I get done today?

What am I grateful for?

How will I win tomorrow?

Date: _____

What did I get done today?

What am I grateful for?

How will I win tomorrow?

Date: _____

What did I get done today?

What am I grateful for?

How will I win tomorrow?

Date: _____

What did I get done today?

What am I grateful for?

How will I win tomorrow?

Date: _____

What did I get done today?

What am I grateful for?

How will I win tomorrow?

Date: _____

What did I get done today?

What am I grateful for?

How will I win tomorrow?

Date: _____

What did I get done today?

What am I grateful for?

How will I win tomorrow?

Date: _____

What did I get done today?

What am I grateful for?

How will I win tomorrow?

Date: _____

What did I get done today?

What am I grateful for?

How will I win tomorrow?

Date: _____

What did I get done today?

What am I grateful for?

How will I win tomorrow?

Date: _____

What did I get done today?

What am I grateful for?

How will I win tomorrow?

Date: _____

What did I get done today?

What am I grateful for?

How will I win tomorrow?

Date: _____

What did I get done today?

What am I grateful for?

How will I win tomorrow?

Date: _____

What did I get done today?

What am I grateful for?

How will I win tomorrow?

Date: _____

What did I get done today?

What am I grateful for?

How will I win tomorrow?

Date: _____

What did I get done today?

What am I grateful for?

How will I win tomorrow?

Date: _____

What did I get done today?

What am I grateful for?

How will I win tomorrow?

Date: _____

What did I get done today?

What am I grateful for?

How will I win tomorrow?

Date: _____

What did I get done today?

What am I grateful for?

How will I win tomorrow?

Date: _____

What did I get done today?

What am I grateful for?

How will I win tomorrow?

Date: _____

What did I get done today?

What am I grateful for?

How will I win tomorrow?

Date: _____

What did I get done today?

What am I grateful for?

How will I win tomorrow?

Date: _____

What did I get done today?

What am I grateful for?

How will I win tomorrow?

Date: _____

What did I get done today?

What am I grateful for?

How will I win tomorrow?

Date: _____

What did I get done today?

What am I grateful for?

How will I win tomorrow?

Date: _____

What did I get done today?

What am I grateful for?

How will I win tomorrow?

Date: _____

What did I get done today?

What am I grateful for?

How will I win tomorrow?

Date: _____

What did I get done today?

What am I grateful for?

How will I win tomorrow?

Date: _____

What did I get done today?

What am I grateful for?

How will I win tomorrow?

Date: _____

What did I get done today?

What am I grateful for?

How will I win tomorrow?

Date: _____

What did I get done today?

What am I grateful for?

How will I win tomorrow?

Date: _____

What did I get done today?

What am I grateful for?

How will I win tomorrow?

Date: _____

What did I get done today?

What am I grateful for?

How will I win tomorrow?

Date: _____

What did I get done today?

What am I grateful for?

How will I win tomorrow?

Date: _____

What did I get done today?

What am I grateful for?

How will I win tomorrow?

Date: _____

What did I get done today?

What am I grateful for?

How will I win tomorrow?

Date: _____

What did I get done today?

What am I grateful for?

How will I win tomorrow?

Date: _____

What did I get done today?

What am I grateful for?

How will I win tomorrow?

Date: _____

What did I get done today?

What am I grateful for?

How will I win tomorrow?

Date: _____

What did I get done today?

What am I grateful for?

How will I win tomorrow?

Date: _____

What did I get done today?

What am I grateful for?

How will I win tomorrow?

Date: _____

What did I get done today?

What am I grateful for?

How will I win tomorrow?

Date: _____

What did I get done today?

What am I grateful for?

How will I win tomorrow?

Date: _____

What did I get done today?

What am I grateful for?

How will I win tomorrow?

Date: _____

What did I get done today?

What am I grateful for?

How will I win tomorrow?

Date: _____

What did I get done today?

What am I grateful for?

How will I win tomorrow?

Date: _____

What did I get done today?

What am I grateful for?

How will I win tomorrow?

Date: _____

What did I get done today?

What am I grateful for?

How will I win tomorrow?

Date: _____

What did I get done today?

What am I grateful for?

How will I win tomorrow?

Date: _____

What did I get done today?

What am I grateful for?

How will I win tomorrow?

Date: _____

What did I get done today?

What am I grateful for?

How will I win tomorrow?

Date: _____

What did I get done today?

What am I grateful for?

How will I win tomorrow?

Date: _____

What did I get done today?

What am I grateful for?

How will I win tomorrow?

Date: _____

What did I get done today?

What am I grateful for?

How will I win tomorrow?

Date: _____

What did I get done today?

What am I grateful for?

How will I win tomorrow?

Date: _____

What did I get done today?

What am I grateful for?

How will I win tomorrow?

Date: _____

What did I get done today?

What am I grateful for?

How will I win tomorrow?

Date: _____

What did I get done today?

What am I grateful for?

How will I win tomorrow?

Date: _____

What did I get done today?

What am I grateful for?

How will I win tomorrow?

Date: _____

What did I get done today?

What am I grateful for?

How will I win tomorrow?

Date: _____

What did I get done today?

What am I grateful for?

How will I win tomorrow?

Date: _____

What did I get done today?

What am I grateful for?

How will I win tomorrow?

Date: _____

What did I get done today?

What am I grateful for?

How will I win tomorrow?

Date: _____

What did I get done today?

What am I grateful for?

How will I win tomorrow?

Date: _____

What did I get done today?

What am I grateful for?

How will I win tomorrow?

Date: _____

What did I get done today?

What am I grateful for?

How will I win tomorrow?

Date: _____

What did I get done today?

What am I grateful for?

How will I win tomorrow?

Date: _____

What did I get done today?

What am I grateful for?

How will I win tomorrow?

Date: _____

What did I get done today?

What am I grateful for?

How will I win tomorrow?

Date: _____

What did I get done today?

What am I grateful for?

How will I win tomorrow?

Date: _____

What did I get done today?

What am I grateful for?

How will I win tomorrow?

Date: _____

What did I get done today?

What am I grateful for?

How will I win tomorrow?

Date: _____

What did I get done today?

What am I grateful for?

How will I win tomorrow?

Final Thoughts: The Journey is the Destination

As a kid, I wasn't much into *Star Trek*, but I was fascinated by the idea of teleportation.

Beam me up!

It's so elegantly efficient; I mean, who wouldn't want to skip all the transit time and instead just instantly arrive where you need to go?

I was all about the destination, and would have been happy skipping the journey entirely.

Are we there yet?

It's taken me a long time to realize this, but **there is no "there."**

The journey *is* the destination.

We've been conditioned to strive toward a number of destinations in our lives:

- Finish high school.
- Graduate from college.
- Get a job.
- Get married.
- Buy a house.
- Start a family.
- Go on vacation.
- Start a business.
- Lose weight.
- Quit your job.
- Retire.

But you know what we find each time we get "there"?

More journey.

In mountain climbing, we call that a false summit.

Even retirement. Every destination—every single one—is greeted with the same question: **"now what?"**

(Only one destination is certain, and it's universal across all ages, races, and nationalities. It's that pesky issue that—not to get too morbid here—ALL our journeys have a 100% mortality rate.)

So what does this have to do with entrepreneurship and productivity?

A lot!

This isn't a call to stop and smell the roses, but it is a reminder that no matter where you are today in terms of your business, you're on the path. You're making progress; moving forward.

Even the people who've supposedly "arrived" **don't see it that way,** so you shouldn't either.

Now, I'm all for setting goals. After all, if you don't know where you're going, how are you going to know how to get there?

But I'm coming to see them more as **milestones rather than endpoints,** because the journey doesn't stop there.

And here's the best part: since the journey *is* the destination, you get to choose your own adventure every day and embrace it as a destination on its own.

After all, your whole life has led you to this day.

Reframed through that lens, challenges and barriers that stand in your way become little **mini-quests to conquer.** That doesn't mean it's always going to be easy or fun (it's not), but it does allow you to be proactive and positive about the journey.

Have you heard this quote from Jon Acuff?

"Don't compare your beginning to someone else's middle."

There's a reason he didn't say "someone else's finish line." Because it's *all* middle.

Keep the Conversation Going

If you'd like to join a supportive and active community of other entrepreneurs and side hustlers, please join the free Side Hustle Nation Facebook group:

SideHustleNation.com/fb

You'll be able to ask questions, help others on their journey, and share your victories along the way.

Liked the Journal?

If you liked this journal, it would mean the world to me if you took a moment to leave an honest review on Amazon. Thank you!

You can also grab your next copy at 3QuestionJournal.com.

Claim Your Free Bonuses

In the spirit of improving not just your productivity, but your overall effectiveness, I put together an exclusive bonus package for users of *The 3 Question Journal.*

1. The Productivity Tip Sheet

I asked some of my most successful entrepreneurial friends for their favorite productivity tips and tricks.

The result is this Tip Sheet.

I don't expect you to try all of these–especially not all at once–but use the suggestions on this list to re-energize and re-focus.

2. The Digital 3 Question Journal

Several readers requested a digital version of the journal to use with their tablet and stylus. If you're embracing a paperless lifestyle, this one is for you.

Plus, it includes 2 extra months of digital pages.

Grab them both free here:

3QuestionJournal.com/bonus

About the Author

Nick Loper is an online entrepreneur and lifelong student in the game of business. He lives in the beautiful Pacific Northwest with his wife Bryn, two sons, and a lovable giant Shih-Tzu called Mochi.

On a typical day you can find him working on his latest business idea, recording another episode of the award-winning Side Hustle Show podcast, rooting for the Huskies, or skiing the Cascade pow.

Nick has witnessed the power of tracking his progress on meaningful projects many times over, until it finally hit him that he should write a book about it.

As you can probably tell from the book, he gets really excited about this stuff and wants to help others find success online.

Want to know more?

Drop by and check out his blog and podcast at SideHustleNation.com, a growing resource and community for aspiring and part-time entrepreneurs.

Connect with fellow side hustlers to share wins, get feedback, and support each in the free Facebook group:

SideHustleNation.com/fb

Do you have a success story to share? Get in touch (nick@sidehustlenation.com)!

Also by Nick

Nick is also the author of:

$1,000 100 Ways: How Real People Make Real Money on the Side (and how you can too)

Buy Buttons: The Fast-Track Strategy to Make Extra Money and Start a Business in Your Spare Time

The Side Hustle: How to Turn Your Spare Time into $1000 a Month or More

The Small Business Website Checklist: A 51-Point Guide to Build Your Online Presence The Smart Way

Virtual Assistant: The Ultimate Guide to Finding, Hiring, and Working with Virtual Assistants

Work Smarter: 500+ Online Resources Today's Top Entrepreneurs Use to Increase Productivity and Achieve Their Goals

37148604R00076